Apollo Lives Here

Mary Green

ISBN: Softcover   978-1-9845-6091-9
        EBook   978-1-9845-6090-2

Print information available on the last page

Rev. date: 11/09/2018

To order additional copies of this book, contact:
Xlibris
1-888-795-4274
www.Xlibris.com
Orders@Xlibris.com

Point of Interest:

I believe in signs. I'm the person who sees a bird fly by and notices if it is a pigeon or a blackbird and feels whether I'm going to hear good news or bad news. That's me. In any case I see the sign. I feel the joy and the sadness that all of life has to offer. So when I received a call and an email from Jen Heavens with Xlibris on the one year anniversary of Apollo's move to the beyond, I saw it as a sign to get this book written and published. Of course, it would be different now. I would have to rewrite it. But that was fine and it was perfect timing for me to celebrate his life and for healing to take place.

APOLLO LIVES HERE

by

Mary Green

This was always going to be the title. Through all the old manuscripts and attempts at writing this book; it was always going to be "Apollo Lives Here". Only now I see his paw print inside my heart. Now I feel the pain of release and the love of freedom - his and mine.

His journey was a precarious one from birth until about 9 or 10 months old when he found me. Some very nice people who were living in their car knew it was best for Apollo and the Great Dane occupying a portion of the back seat, for them both to find shelter and new permanent homes. I'm sure that was a hard decision not one that I could have easily made either.

But the journey wasn't over finding a home. Apollo and I would move again and again. I could blame my non-committal sensibility or I could just blame society. Or maybe it wasn't in the stars. It was not for lack of trying since I truly wanted the little house and white picket fence as well. I thought about making a sign for him that said "Apollo Lives Here" and posting it in the yard at a house we had a few years back. It would seem that was *not to be* either. Yet, my boy stayed with me and went everywhere with me through thick and thin. He loved me and always greeted me with a smile in the morning and at the door when I came home – just as long as he got a bone LOL!

A New Name: At first thought, when I saw him: "He's way too big. He's Huge". But actually he saw me first; stopped in his tracks stared into my eyes and ran right over to me wearing a big smile. I tried to push him away but his fur was so soft that my fingers slipped right through him like wearing a silicone glove. He stood his ground - solid as a butcher block. Nose in face – UGH Dog Breath. That's a smell you never forget. Maneuvering into my sights he landed his head on my lap. Still I resisted with all my strength until the very forward big wet kiss right on my mouth.

"The problem is I'm just visiting here for now and I know you are too but I kinda have to have a place to take you home to - ya know dawg"

No, He never listened to me. On point, he was the man of me from the start not letting anyone else get too close. I completely understood since he had been kicked around from house to home. The last family left him outdoors *ALONE* while they went on their Vegas Vacay. When they got home and saw he ate all the lawn furniture, they got mad and took him to the shelter. It was a Saturday Morning and the Shelter was CLOSED. Lucky Dog! Then they brought him to my brother's house, of course. My sister-n-law said "yes" to everyone (and still does). At that point they were planning to send him up North to someone's farm. I could see he had been pushed around too much and that's when I put my foot down and said: "NO, I'm taking him.

He's my dog now'. After that, no one got involved - since being on the opposite end of my anger was not a good place to be *ever*.

I will never forget the way he walked in the front door through the living room and the dinning room – then planted himself on the kitchen floor. He stood right behind me not making a sound while I washed the dishes. When I turned around he was just sitting there staring up at me. I jumped and caught myself; said hello and gave him a big bear hug around his neck. I realized he'd lost weight since the last time I saw him and he waaas hungreee. He went through three big bowls of dog food and 5 water bowls. Then out in the yard for a romp and a dump.

His head was bigger than my bottom and he loved chasing it. His tail curled up ever so slightly – not that of a Husky – but more dangerous and noisy in the hallway. The kitchen sink he swallowed explained the steel well and immovable force throughout his casing. There really was no guessing how much he weighed in at with all the fluffy fur flowing from his back. He certainly looked like a white German Shepard but he had some other mix that was

hard to detect. What caught me though was his eyes. They still captivate me and always will. They were Almond shaped, deep brown outlined in black with white lashes. I tried not to look straight into his eyes. It was truly as if he'd known me before and he knew me now and would be with me forever and day.

He played in spontaneous bursts of energy that lasted 5 to 10 minutes. Thank goodness. I couldn't take much more than that. Then he would flop down wherever and look at me with his eyes and mouth wide open panting. Like "Did you see that?"

"Yes, I saw that"; myself smiling from ear to ear. I took so much pleasure in watching his happy time..He was just a puppy with big boy paws and he really really wanted to play. Watching him run with his head held high into the wind that swirled around him stopped me and gave me chills. He looked like a marble statue that came to life. The easiest and hardest thing was naming him. The name he'd been given was all wrong for him and I won't repeat it. He needed a name to fit his personality and his appearance. A name fit for a God: "Apollo" it is. And he truly lived up to his name.

He Took the Lead: The first thing I did after deciding he was staying with me, was to buy him a collar and tether. I would not hear any more talk of shelters or other peoples homes who were *not* home. It was decided. Apollo was staying with me from now on. I mean when a dog walks through the front door, struts through the living room and dining room and sits his butt down behind you in the kitchen while your washing dishes, you know only one thing - *He's hungry and he expects you to feed him for free for the rest of his life* - So I did.

Our first walk down the street went well actually. I had to get comfortable holding a thick giant rope as a leash. Big Dog – Big Leash. That's when it started, from that very first walk together. People noticed us – *him* – Apollo. Its not every day you see a huge white dog pulling a little lady down the street. And of course I got the jokes about who's walking who? Everyone wanted to see him and talk to him. We got stopped a lot. He was not pretty, he was beautiful. He was a giant ball of fur and proudly wore his coat in the winter, summer, fall or spring. Sorry if he left a few fur balls in your yard. He was always shedding. No there was no cat mix in him – just some cat nip. The slightest noise from a car door slamming or junk in a garage down the street falling would set him off. You would laugh to see him jump 2 feet in the air and turn all the way around to see what the noise was. Still nothing deterred him from patrolling his walk-path that he chose.

He was at my side as expected just at my left hip. The rope slung down from my left hand over to the right so I could keep control of the distance he strode. He took to the choker like it was jewelry - which by the way really doesn't choke a dog and you don't have to be Wonder Woman to hold on. Just take the leash with choker attached and pull up from the neck. It will hold your dog in place in the moment as needed: such as chasing a car driving by or kid on a bicycle or another dog jumping out from behind a neighbors bush because you are in *their* front yard. Yes, we braved the neighborhood street boldly together. Back in the house for a treat and a little playtime. It was always playtime for Apollo until he was tired.

The first stuffed animal toy I bought Apollo was Mr. Quackers, a duck that made quacking noises when you squeezed it. Apollo did that with his big teeth, then handed it to me to squeeze it for him. That's when you know it's true love... when your dawg slobers all over his favorite toy and then drops it in your lap to play with him. Yep, no doubt that is true love in the rarest form. Watching him, I expected him to rip it apart, but he didn't. He just licked it to death. Ok, it was already dead - I mean not alive. Apollo thought it was and he made friends with Mr. Quackers. He took care of it and slept with it and played with it and wouldn't let me near it. We then started a collection of stuffed toys from the grocery store: Sally the Squirrel, Lamby and Moooo Cow. So he not only expected his milkbones when I came home, he also expected a toy. Yep, I did that...

Moving Day: Looking back on moving day is always much easier than going through it. Conversely looking forward to moving day is the worst most absolute feeling in the entire world since there is no place in this world where moving day is a breeze. I loved that third floor apartment with the balcony and fireplace. It was perfect for us. Just a roomy one bedroom where Apollo could run from living room to bedroom, jump in the bed and wait for me to find him. The minute I did and ducked my head moving right to left catching his eye, that was his Que to jump out of bed and run back in the living room. Every once in awhile I left him on the bed hoping he'd forget to find me. Eventually, he would tire himself out and then drink a full bowl of water – wait for me to fill it up again and then he was happy. *Really Dawg!*

Oh but how I loved my Apollo. I could watch him for hours. I kept the balcony door open so he could go outside and come back in when he was ready. He always had to have one eye on me. We were high enough to see the birds in the trees and be able to look down on people coming and going. Of course he barked at every other dog that walked by. He was doing his job and at the same time I knew he just wanted to play. There was so much Peace here. I'm a people watcher so checking out the scene was perfect for me too. This was an ideal setting for us both.

The surrounding area had a field to the back of the apartment complex that was fenced in for the kids to play. And further beyond that was a neighborhood with a little park and trees where you could just walk into the woods. So Apollo's walk grew into something much bigger. His world was open to greater possibilities and adventures. He did not want to come back from his walk. He wanted to keep walking and discovering new places. That's when he got stubborn with me. That was the first time he took hold of his tether (the thick rope kind); put it in-between his teeth and kept walking in his own direction. He picked his head up, looked back at me with a sideways glance and his eyes were bugged out and rolling up at me. Okay, I've said it before and I guess I just have to keep saying it. *Really Dawg!* He was totally the man of me and he was letting me know it.

NO, Don't Jump. Most people say "Don't Jump". I never told him that unless there were other people in the room. I loved it when he jumped up to meet me face to face. He was happy and excited. He always got in at least two or three good ones before calming down so I could stroke his fur; hug his big thick neck and play with his ears. And OH, how he loved his kisses. So, I didn't tell him to stop licking either. Right in my face with mouth open – HIS – not mine. LOL! I had a friend from work come over one time and she told me I was going too far. I didn't respond. I just smiled. I never changed and hoped he would not either – he didn't. The jumping; the licking; the playtime. I wanted it to last forever.

He had this football thing going on. No, I don't know anything about the game; but *he* did to the point where I thought he might have been a football player in a past life or maybe the people who had him before taught him how to score a touchdown. He did with me. I thought he must have learned it from somewhere or someone. I realized it the first time he shouldered me from behind. We were

running around in the back yard at my brothers house when he circled me then jumped me from behind hitting my shoulder almost knocking me down. I was pretty shocked but not scared. Then he hunched down on his two front paws with butt up in the air. Truly a sight to behold. He looked me straight me in the eye as if he was saying: "Here I am, come and get me." I met his challenge. I hunched down – elbows on my upper legs – looked him back in the eye – moved my head from right to left and it was on. That's right. We were playing football without the ball. I made him chase me dodging out of the way. I'm not stupid. Fool me once – not twice. Then I just had to buy him one of those soft fuzzy squeezy footballs. I found out fast he didn't like the plastic ones. He just wanted the soft kind that made noise when he chomped down on it. He added that football to his treasure trove of toys not to be washed or moved out of his sight.

Hmmmm. Still a puppy and growing with a tremendous need for love and attention, I realized he was suffering from separation anxiety. My job was close by, so I would come home at lunch to walk him and make sure he had enough water. He really only ate once a day at that point (as long as he got a cookie in-between meals). So, I thought I was taking good care of him. I truly hated leaving him alone for any length of time; but you have to work to buy the bones doggie dog. Get it. When he was younger I used to call him Doggie Dog. I'd say "Want to go for a Walkie Walk Doggie Dog". He *knew* what I was saying. He could be resting totally in front of the cold fireplace and then jump 5 ½ feet in the air. Just over my head and away we went.

So, one day I came home from work at the end of the day expecting him to greet me at the door and he wasn't there. The first thing I saw was yellow wrapper on the floor. I'm thinking: "What is this". Picked up the first piece and realized it was my potato chips bag ripped to shreds. "How did he get it. Where is he"?? I went in my bedroom and there he was laying on the bed with his head down, his two paws underneath his chin just waiting for me to say something. I didn't say a word. What do you say. He didn't do that because he was hungry. He did it because he saw me eating the potato chips and put them back in the pantry – on the top shelf I might add – and he wanted what I had. So I started putting the chips on top of the fridge knowing he couldn't jump that high. I was afraid he'd knock the refrigerator down on it's side though. He was strong enough to do that. But he never got the fridge doors to open – Thank God for small favors and big wonders.

Leaving him alone all day long for hours on end was out of the question. I broke it down to two or three hours at a time (disregarding work schedule). It was a Sunday and I had been reading my bible which I do on the occasion. I put it back on my nightstand said my goodbyes see you later and off I went to church thinking he'll be fine for a couple of hours. When I came home I found my bible on the bed right where I had been reading it that morning. The bottom right corner had been nibbled. I realized he saw me reading, waited till I left picked it up off the nightstand and proceeded to gnaw into it. But then he stopped for some unknown reason. It was as if he knew he should respect my most loved possession or it was somehow holy. This time he was in the living room waiting. He had that look on his face *again* and he didn't meet me at the door. So I knew something was up when I came in. I really couldn't say another word to him. That one is an enigma to this day. I love you Apollo...

That was the start of a life long habit of Apollo's. He ignored as he had so many times before and put his nose in my purse. I had holy bread there from church. He did not stop digging until he got it out. Now mind you his mouth was bigger than my purse and how he got it out still baffles me. That dog found food anywhere. So then he knew when Church day came around every a week and that I would be bringing him home a treat in my purse that he so loved. I began saying prayers over him when I gave him the bread in a little sort of chanting tone: "Holy Bread for the Holy Dog from Hea- ven", with emphasis on Heaven.

I've always had a twang of guilt about that. I don't think you're supposed to give your holy bread to your dog. But still I think God understands. I know Apollo is in Doggie Heaven. He's my angel.

Dog Fight: "I'm going to a Barbecue tonight. I won't be long. Just a couple of hours. So you be good". I know that's how the conversation went while Apollo sat upright staring into my eyes. When I was done talking he turned his head. He always did that. The weird part is I know he knew what I was saying; but he didn't want to hear it so he acted stupid. It was all just an act.

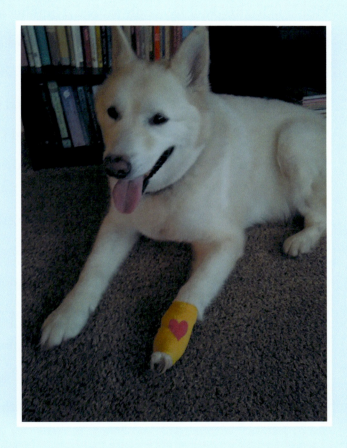

Out for a last minute walk around the complex so I wouldn't have to worry about him which I did anyway. We didn't take our normal route since this was a short one. It was still nice and peaceful despite the traffic of people coming and going. It was fall now and the air shifted ever so slightly a few degrees. I love it when the air changes just enough to feel the new season approaching. It's exciting to think of newness blowing in. The complex was large enough to make it an interesting walk nonetheless. He was never disappointed nor was I with the winding pathways in and around the buildings and the grounds.

On our way back – a short walk this time. We were just at the bottom of the steps. Reminder 3rd floor. About two steps up, when a dog ran out from behind us and jumped on Apollo's back. I screamed. Apollo went into full dog force. I was trying to hold him back; but he was on it. In retrospect I should have let go of his leash. He would have stood a better chance defending himself and me. The problem was the other dog - was smaller and faster. I couldn't stop screaming. I didn't know how to stop them from fighting. I totally freaked out. A lady walking by heard the fight and jumped in to stop the dogs. She got hurt pretty bad. One of the dogs bit her on the arm; but she stopped the fight. Thank God for that Dear Woman. To this day I feel badly for her. Thinking about that moment makes me shiver. She called an ambulance and they took her in for stitches. The police came and so did the Animal Protective People. It was determined that the fault of the fight was the other dog *NOT APOLLO*. Apparently, it had jumped out of the first floor window when it saw Apollo and jumped him because he was so big and white. Wait, WHAT! I thought that was a load then and still do. The final conclusion stated Apollo was on a leash with me and the other dog was loose. It was the other dog's fault.

Hours had passed after all the reports were filed, when I noticed some blood on the floor by the fireplace where Apollo laid. I looked at him more closely and he was bleeding out badly. The authorities were still in the parking lot so I went down and told them about Apollo's condition. They told me to take him to the Animal Hospital up the road. I asked for help and then told them I wanted to file a report on Apollo's account and they said no because he's not a human. Excuse ME! That was another pile laid on top of the last load. So, I pulled it together and got him to walk down the stairs with me and got him in the car and drove him to the hospital myself. Tears, Shaking, Horror. Oh no.

What's going to happen to him. "I've only had him six months and I love him and don't want him to die". I don't remember driving there or how I found the place. Just walking in with my boy.

The people at the hospital were really really good. Of course, I did not have insurance for him; but they signed us up on the spot. They don't turn anyone away. They took Apollo in to the examining room to assess his wounds. I'll never forget him looking back at me. He was scared. He had never really been to the Vet before. When I first got him, I took him to the Pet Store for his shots and supplies and that was it. I could see he was not happy – mouth closed, ears down, eyes droopy, tail motionless. They wouldn't let me go in there with him otherwise I would have.

Then the attendant approached me in the waiting room with the news of his injuries explaining in full detail the operation he needed to survive; and that he might not survive. He asked me to sign a paper stating if I wanted him to be placed on life support or let him go. I didn't have to think about it. I said "NO, Don't Let Him Die!" More Tears, More Shaking, More Shock! I waited and waited and waited until they got him ready to come home with me. It was very late that night; but he walked out of the hospital by my side – leaving a few presents behind. LOL. They loaded him up with antibiotics and pain pills which I later dubbed "doggie downers". He *loved* them and he knew which one it was. There was nothing dumb about that dog.

"God as my witness, I will never have another apartment on the third floor. Oh man!" Getting that dog to go up and down the stairs every day with the head gear on him and the bandages around his two front legs was hell to pay. Apollo had 80 bite marks on his back. I counted them. The under part of his front legs were ripped open. He had to have sutures and we had to be careful of infection setting in – so I needed to check it frequently and squeeze that area to make sure it was draining properly and not collecting fluids.

At the time, He weighed in at about 109 pounds. He then gained 10 pounds. That's when I started taking him to the Vet on a regular basis. I had to really. He truly hated it. He always thought I was going to leave him there and I'm sure he had bad memories of that night associated to the examining room. The good part is I was able to be with him full time. So we got through it. He totally milked the extra love and attention from me. I used to put his pills in meat kabobs or bread squeezies. It was better than potato chips. The antibiotics tasted bad. He had a hard time getting those down. But I made him take every last pill. Normally it just went down the back of his throat without much of a chew so I wondered how he knew how it tasted. Maybe it was more of a smell thing.

I grappled with the Apartment complex about the situation and they would do nothing about it. I wanted them to remove that dog or something. I know they were fined but that didn't seem like it was enough. That wasn't the biggest problem on my plate though. Bills were piling up. I lost yet another job from staying home with Apollo to nurse his wounds in the middle of a recession. In all fairness they told me I could bring him to work with me. But, I couldn't see it. He was WAAAAY Too Big for that small office. I eventually found work in retail during the holiday season. Not what I wanted to do – but we do what we have to sometimes. Yet again timing was not on my side. The Apartments said they would work with me on the rent. That was not so true. It's a really bad feeling when you're leaving home to go to work and turn around to close the door and find an eviction notice there. That is not a good feeling. We had to move *again*.

We went through a few roommates. I can still recall people saying: "We'll take you but not the dog"; or just the opposite: "We'll take the dog but not you". Yes that stung. There would be no separating us. We were glued to each other. Until the day came when I found a house just for us.

Our House was a very very very fine house. With two cats in the yard. Life used to be soooo hard – Until I found *one* dog named Apollo. Thank you "Crosby, Stills, Nash and Young". I love that song. Now everything is easy cause of youuuuuuuu.........

"Okay, it's a bit of a fixer upper and it may take me a little longer to get all the work done; but it's ours. Just you and me all alone. No Roommates or anyone else. I own it or at least there's just a small mortgage on it that I'm sure I can take care of for us. It's perfect. Two Bedrooms Two Baths. Not Too Big. Not Too Small. A fenced in back yard.

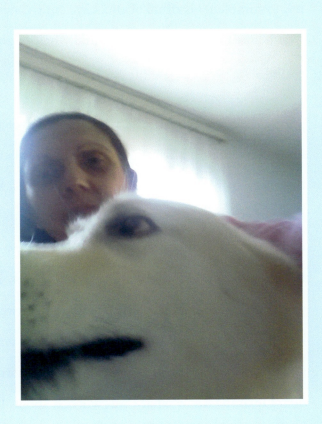

There is a screened in porch with a concrete patio next to it to give you a bath. I know that's a dirty word. Sorry. Tile flooring all throughout the house. Better for my allergies and for you to lay down anywhere you want. The neighborhood is a little rough in some areas but the people next door on both sides look good. That makes all the difference in the world - having good neighbors. "Are you with me on this dawg?" The run through and around the house from side to side answered that question.

5:45 am; shoes, socks, shirt, pants, tether, dog and out the door for a walk. How did we ever start this ridiculous habit. But that dog had to have his walk first thing in the morning before I even had my tea. I thought now that we have a yard he can just go in the back; but noooooo – not him. He has to complete his ritual of checking out the neighborhood and all the houses and comings and goings first before anything else. He actually had to go doggie dump at least 3 times every morning. He had an outrageous constitution.

You would think he was the leader of the Neighborhood Watch Program. "Yo Dawg, they don't have one in this neighborhood." It was a slight saving grace that Apollo wasn't walking far distances at this point, so I never actually took him around the block. I went down our street reading some of the names on the mailboxes: one said "killer", and we crossed the street. There were a few houses being renovated and that's always a good sign. But, he would go just so far and then stop along the way and sit like this is a good spot to reflect on life. He was tired and … ran out of steam. It was perfectly normal for *him*. He didn't know what I was worried about. I would be making faces and smiling and pulling on his collar and walking backward looking at him and he would just turn his head from side to side – like: "what's wrong with her?" "Really Dawg!"

We had a beautiful old tree in the front yard. It was a flowering tree that had been there for forty years. It was gorgeous. It was *the* selling point of the house – bigger than the house tree. I loved that tree. It was home to many a birds. Mainly pigeons. The back yard was overgrown with trees and bushes. I had red birds of every kind in my yard. They used to perch on the window sill outside the bedroom window. So I started feeding them bird seed with a clean water bowl. We woke up every morning to the song of birds. Apollo could sit there for hours and watch the birds and listen to them talk to each other. He never once chased them.

He did eat a turtle once, I must confess. I can talk about it now that he's gone. I felt so guilty when he did it at the time. I just did not see that turtle go into the yard. It was a large land turtle and they are everywhere. Most of the time we are all very aware of turtles and allow them to cross the road undisturbed (no matter how long it takes). But this guy just walked right into the back yard – probably for the grass and bushes – right under the fence and was just gonna keep going into the next yard – I'm sure – until Apollo spotted him. It was too late then. I was in the house just keeping an eye out for him in the backyard when I looked at him and he looked at me straight in the eyes with his mouth closed and there appeared to be blood on his chin. Hard to miss that on a white dog. So I quickly went out there; but by the time I got to him he had this thing in his mouth that looked like a steak from far away. As I got closer I saw a hard shell, four little legs and no head. He was holding it in his mouth looking up at me.

"LET IT GO - NOW!" I had to repeat myself several times and grab him by the collar. He had no idea what he had done wrong. This was the most delicious dinner he had ever had. I'm sure he thought it was a delicacy. Turtle Soup, of course! Eventually, he got my meaning. I dragged him into the house and closed the sliding glass doors behind me as I proceeded with caution towards the recently deceased Mr. Turtle. *He never had a stuffed toy friend like that. Maybe if I had bought him one, he might not have eaten it.* I wanted to bury it with dignity and a ceremony and everything to honor it's life and long line of ancestors. But, that would not have worked since Apollo would have dug him up and finished his dinner. So, I did the safe thing. Yes I did. I had to. I love turtles...

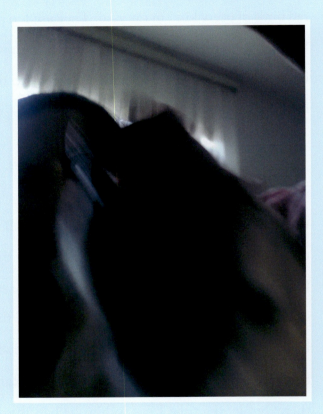

Puddle Jumper: "It's raining, No we can't go out now. It's very very wet outside. It's been raining all night and it's probably gonna rain all day. I'll keep an eye on the weather and as soon as it let's up - even a little, we can go out, OKAY!"

Apollo stared out the window from the front room then pulled himself up and walked to the back patio. Put his nose out the door and looked up at the trees. Not even the birds were out playing. His mouth was closed and had droopy eyes looking at me like "Mommy can't you make it stop raining". OMGeeeee talk about a broken heart. That dog could win the medal of honor for empathy. If you weren't feeling it, he would make you feel it. And he knew I wouldn't let him go out in the back yard with it sopping wet, so he stood there sulking. The couch was his favorite spot for looking out the front window. He leaned on the armrest and laid his body over the large pillows. It was just high enough for him to see what was going on without lifting his head up. All he had to do was move his eyes back and forth and his head followed.

Don't ya know the minute the downpour stopped he was ready for a walkie walk. "Ok, doggie dog – let's go now before it starts up again." Just like a miracle happened, he jumped up from the couch and was in my face smiling with big eyes trying to jump up to meet me like he did as a puppy. So I got his tether and out we went to brave the impending tundra. He was ready for anything – four foot paws, two ears, big nose and flying tail. I tried to walk him in the middle of the street to avoid the puddles (more like flood waters), but that did not work. He looked down at the water and put all four paws right in it and stomped up and down making bigger splashes each time. "Really Dawg, did you have to do that". Of Course, he did. Then I pulled him up on the grass, which I was trying to avoid because it was all so wet, but I knew he wouldn't go in the street. He had to have big soft grass and find the right spot. "Seriously, I'm tellin you" Then he took off for the bushes that were just the right height to hit the top of his back. He totally enjoyed the cool water dropping on his nose and butt at the same time. He then got under the bushes and walked back and forth and looked at me with a big Thank You Smile. I couldn't help but smile back. Apollo was just a big kid – a puppy with big boy paws. Time to go back in. Yep, wet dirty floors. I just smiled. He loved it when I got out his big bath towel with black, gray and white stripes. He knew that was his. I draped it over his back and got his ears first then under his chin and worked my way down to his tail. The legs and paw paws were always last. Then I sopped up the water from the floor with the dirty doggie towel – then the washer. Yep! "I Love You and Miss You Apollo. Thank you for teaching me to walk in the rain."

Flying High: From the very first ride in the car, I realized he was a natural. I was afraid he'd get sick and throw up in the back seat; but not Apollo. He loved to go for a ride in the car. It was as if he was in an airplane. Time had no time for us when were flying around. Window open - head perched up - nose out – wind in your face; the colder the better. He was a Fall, Winter and Spring Dog. Yes, the summer months were fine; but you'd find him inside the AC with his nose to the window. It was too hot for him. So, we drove around at night during summer months when the sun went down.

I was totally accustomed to people stopping us as we walked down the street. Oftentimes, people stopped their cars driving by and yelled out the window to tell me how beautiful he was. We would always stop to talk and smile. Apollo loved meeting new people. And he was loved. I didn't expect the same when we were driving around. Of course, I'm trying to keep my eye on the road in front of me and one eye in the rear view mirror just watching him. Then there'd be a little kid in a car in the next lane staring at Apollo and smiling, waving and talking to him. That was always fun. He loved that.

The biggest thrill was driving through the park. He watched all the trees stream by him right before his eyes with the wind in his face as if he were flying from tree to tree with the birds. He could not get enough of nature. He could ride for hours and hours. Not me, when it was time to go home – it was time. I told myself he can't tell time, he's a dog. I think I read that somewhere. But anyway, sigh. It's all right. He got his rides in from puppydom to senior stardom. I remember him jumping in the back seat and then trying to jump in the front seat and back again. He was just too big to fit – he would have if he could have. Then I was helping him get in with a boost up from behind. That's love – picking up a 150 pound dog from the back end to get him in the car for a ride. Especially on the last one.

Meet Jack: That night it was dead silent in the neighborhood. Apollo and I were just sitting at the table talking and playing when he jumped up and ran in the back yard. I didn't know what he was running for. I thought it might have been a opossum or something. He smells critters coming. Then I saw another big white dog on the other side of the fence and thought I was seeing a reflection of Apollo only thinner and younger. Those two were nose to nose at the fence and not barking. Both tails were wagging and I had no idea where this other big white dog came from. Until I saw a flashlight heading in our direction with a man holding it. We said hello. He introduced himself and his dog. Apparently, they were just moving in and the electricity was not turned on yet. I wondered. I'm always a little leery of people at first until I see what is for myself.

The house behind ours had been empty for a few months and they had been working on it night and day fixing the roof and painting and getting it ready. So now the new owner was moving in at night with no power. Poor guy had to sleep in his van with his dog. They got everything up and running the next morning; but still. That's not what you want to walk into. So he said: "Meet Jack" I don't know what kind of dog he was. Apollo was a white German Shepard mix – you could tell by his ears and big nose. "Brothers from another mother" was all his owner could say. I just smiled. We would soon become friends and there was no stopping these two from budding up with each other. Jack was spry and fit. So, Apollo just watched him after a run or two back and forth. He flipped his body around and sat there watching Jack play the field.

That was until Missy came by to say hello. She was Apollo's girlfriend. She was a teeny tiny little girl and oh so sweet. The first time I saw her at the fence with Apollo I freaked. I couldn't see where he had gone. So I walked around to the side of the house and Missy was right there down at his ankles looking up into his eyes. She probably weighed in at the same of one his paws. She looked to be about 25 pounds and she was walking with her Mommy. We said hello and chatted while the two carried on. It became a daily thing for Missy to see Apollo and get in her sweetness. He would even wait for her at the front door and I'd let him out for a few minutes. He was smitten. And oh so protective. If any other dog walked by our house that was it. Apollo was funny that way either he liked you or he didn't and you knew it.

Window Pain: I was sitting right there. Completely relaxed like nothing was happening. Really not doing anything when all of a sudden out of nowhere Apollo jumped up off the couch and ran over to the front window in two moves was on his hind legs and took his right front paw and tapped it against the window pane shattering it into a million pieces. I was in shock for the first 10 seconds which felt like 10 minutes. Then I jumped to my feet to see what was going on in the front yard. It was just another dog walking by. Yes, I know you don't like him. But, there's nothing we can do about it. People walk by with their dogs the same way I walk you. "Oh My Goodness! What am I going to do now. I'll have to replace the window – that's all" True it was an old Florida Window with really really thin glass; but I wasn't exactly ready to replace it right then.

I watched him do it. I'm still amazed by it. I remembered my brother's words. "That dog would jump through a window for you" I just didn't think those words would come back on me. *Really Dawg.* Thank you brother...

Then the barking – nonstop. Pulling him back off the window sill without hurting him and getting cut from the glass was a magical feat. Apollo was a bleeder that much had already been proven. We don't need to do this part again. So I just put him in my bedroom until I could sweep up all the glass in the front room and outside on the front porch. Then I boarded up that part of the window and; "Oh well sorry, you can't look out the window anymore Dawg!"

After it was all over I felt horrible. I went into the bedroom where he was waiting quietly sitting on my bed looking at me eye spot on - head perched up high - the moment I opened the door. I gave him a big hug and then looked him over nose to tail. I thought for sure he'd have some blood on his paws since I saw some droplets outside on the glass that went flying. He must have licked himself or there really weren't any deep cuts. I think we got lucky that time – that's all. It's a true wonder that dog made it as long as he did. I'm still shaking from that sight in my memory.

Healing: Cosequin, Bayer, Benadryl... The first time I saw Apollo cave in from behind and not be able to pick himself up, my heart broke in a thousand pieces. I cried hysterically. I didn't know what to do for him or what was wrong. He was just getting up to walk across the room and he couldn't – he went back down and then up again and then down. I still feel it and see it.

I talked to enough people who told me stories about their dogs who all suggested Cosequin. It was a real lifesaver; not just for Apollo, but me too. It gave me hope. It worked immediately if not sooner – meaning the first 3 days. I had him on it for the last 5 years of his life. Then I gave him treats to include those with supplements for his hips. Yep, he had a big bum and it was bumpy.

There were really bad days when he wouldn't do anything but lay there. He wouldn't eat and I could barely get him to drink his water. It would pass. I realized that the pain in his two front legs had returned from the old injuries he incurred as a puppy. I guess we would never forget that time. My neighbor suggested I put him on Bayer Aspirin. So, I did and that seemed to help.

Apollo did not like the Vet. I took him in when I had to; but not on a regular basis. I learned to take care of him myself on my own which I wouldn't suggest – but hey you do what you have to do. It was what he needed.

The itchies is what got me. I thought it had to be something in that back yard with all the foliage. But then I realized a dog will bite the area of pain he's in because he doesn't know what else to do. It hurts so he bites it. He bit up his hind legs. And then he got a rash there. A friend told me to try benadryl and that worked also. Apollo was falling apart. Seriously For Real. Right before my eyes and my heart was breaking. I loved him too much and didn't want to let him go. I wanted to turn back time so he could be a puppy again and do things just slightly different to bring a different outcome. I just wanted him with me for another 10 years. Can I clone you Apollo. LOL.

This three ring circus brought me to my brink. So, I placed my hands on him from memory of my old Reiki Class Teachings (that I never used) and prayed really really hard with all my heart. He showed improvement And I kept it up. It's actually hard to explain how healing works and how you know it's working. It's just the day to day scenarios you play. The walk –

the talk – the playtime. It was all just so much more normal. Healing became a regular part of our life. I have healer friends who also sent me energy healing for Apollo (for which I am very grateful) and it worked. There were no more bites on the butt or slips back to the floor trying to get up. No more depression. Yeah, I think he was depressed at times. It added a few more quality years to his life. I would not have done that part differently.

One Day: I woke up and saw Apollo smiling at me from beside the bed. He slowly pulled himself up with his two front paws and then one hind leg at a time. He stood up on my bed and turned around and then around again until he found the right spot and then laid down on top of my legs. *Laughing now with a big smile.* I wrapped my arms around his neck and hugged him ever so gently. He sat perfectly still as he was in the moment as well. This was a lazy morning with nothing to do but be right here. So we laid there for a little while longer. Eventually, we got up – first Apollo then me. It was time. I got dressed, grabbed his tether and we went out for a walk.

It was a beautiful morning. We walked down the street and around the block. He was walking longer distances now in a new neighborhood. The grass is greener on this side. It's perfect in that hour before the sun comes up. It's not too too hot and there is just enough coolness in the air to make it easier to breathe. Apollo stopped along the way at the retention pond to look at the ducks in the water. I let him and just waited until he was ready. And so off we were once again. He found a puddle or two to jump in while I looked at the houses that were previously for sale and now had people living in them. I laughed at his wet paw paws. He looked up at me – pulled his head back up with a big smile and tugged to go this way. I went where he wanted to go. There was always a new tree to discover.

We found our way back home soon enough for a treat. I made my tea while he ate his bone. I stretched out and did my yoga poses while he waited for his friends to walk by the house peering out the front window. I peeled open my banana. Bananas were his favorite. He just waited for me to give him a bite. He liked cold bananas out of the fridge. It always somehow turned into one and half bananas for me and him. He had gotten used to his pills every morning. I made these little doggie meatballs out of canned dog food (that was good for him) He scarfed them down without ever knowing what was in them. He just knew he felt better and the taste going down the back of his throat was most excellent. After breakfast it was then time for his nap. He napped a lot now.

Apollo always woke up in a good mood and happy for the next moment. It was time for a ride. Mid-morning was good for us both. He put his nose up to the car door handle waiting for me to open it for him. Then one front paw and then then the next while I lifted his bottom up and all in. Now he liked sitting more in the middle of the seat where he could be next to me. He was so big that his head fit perfectly over the front console in between the driver and passenger seats. It's like he was driving with me. He'd look straight ahead to see where I was going next. He had his favorite streets and so did I. He loved the little hills and the rolling green grass. Every once in awhile we'd see golfers in their golf carts drive by with their furry friend. He got so excited, I almost got him his own golf cart. But no. That's silly. He got tired and put his head down and I knew when it was time to take him home for another nap.

His favorite food was chicken soup. I took chicken broth and cooked yams – cut them up into Apollo sized bites and mixed it in with his kibbles. OMG, you never saw a dog so happy for his dinner.

Heee loved it. The chicken broth was good for his stomach and the yams were good for his hips. I know he knows now that he knew then just how much I loved him to do all that for his dinner. He knew it.

I laid down on the floor next to him and gave him a full body hug. Apollo was always bigger than me. It just always felt so unusual and safe at the same time when my feet were playing with his tail and my head was smothered in the fur behind his ears. He loved kisses. He was so soft and smooth. He was waiting for his belly rub and I obliged. So if you can picture the Big Boy laying on the floor on his right side and me laying on the floor behind him head to toe – getting kisses and a belly rub and tail fluff all at the same time. You now know how crazy I was for my boy.

"Okay, you want to go for another walk. Ok, Good Boy, Let's Go, Mommy take her boy for a walk". I have no idea why I talked baby talk to grown up dog, but I did it. I think he liked it to. "We can go anywhere you want to go. Ok, you just want to sit here on the grass. That's fine". It didn't take long for the neighbors to come out and say hello to us. Everyone loved Apollo. He was friendly, fun and loving. The lady next door to us had a little yappy dog. Apollo didn't care if it barked. He just ignored it. She was very kind and always kept her dog at bay or would go in a different direction.

Apollo could pick a spot anywhere and be at home. He made friends everywhere he went. The Weatherman was on his side of the cloud. And there was always a silver lining. Ready to go in a split second for a new adventure. Apollo I will love you forever and a day. You taught me how to live. We had each other and that's all either one of us ever needed.

Author's Note I will always be Apollo's Mommy. The paw print he left on my heart and soul has changed me permanently. I know he's waiting for me and will open the gate to our Mansion in Heaven. I hope to spend the rest of my year's here writing and perhaps publishing a few things before I go.

I was born into this world as Mary Green. Through a few name changes of my own (marriage and divorce), I decided simple was best so going back to my authentic self was an easy choice. However, I wished my mother had given me a middle name. Don't get me wrong. Simple is always the easiest thing for me to reckon with. But I truly always wanted a middle name. So, I thought I could name myself keeping my own name in the process.

My mother just wasn't all that creative in 1957. It was tradition to be named after your grandmother. And in my case it was both my grandmothers. So, I am Mary. My brother got my father's first name as his middle name, Richard. And I was always a little jealous of that. But how do you make Richard a girls name. Today we are far more creative with names for which I am grateful. So I thought I could be Richelle after my father as well. Not taking anything away from my baby brother. I'm sure he will approve. So, Mary Richelle Green it is.

Printed in the United States
By Bookmasters